Casey Krysztofik received his bachelor of science degree (cum laude) in Mathematics from Ohio University (USA). Casey also received an associate of dance degree (honours) in American Style Smooth and Rhythm from Dance Vision International Dance Association.

Casey Krysztofik

TANKA CAVALCADE

Referring not to toy
construction trucks

AUSTIN MACAULEY PUBLISHERS™

LONDON * CAMBRIDGE * NEW YORK * SHARJAH

A CIP catalogue record for this title is available from the British Library.

ISBN 9781398442818 (Paperback)
ISBN 9781398443921 (Hardback)
ISBN 9781398444782 (ePub e-book)

www.austinmacauley.com

First Published 2023
Austin Macauley Publishers Ltd®
1 Canada Square
Canary Wharf
London
E14 5AA

I want to thank Joshua Waterfield and the board of editors at Austin Macauley Publishers for their support and confidence in this work.

Table of Contents

Sweet Bay Magnolia

Sun pours smelted gold.
Eyes' swift reject muscle bites
Keen to small spot swab.
Protective shade. Redaction:
Erasure poetry void.

Chrism glow. Minus-
Cule omega curios
Move soul's medulla.
Delicate male anuran
Pouch full blazoned intumesce.

Boutonniere centre
Piece. Kunik: slow bee collects
Pollen pendulum.
Fool for vacuuming morsels…
Found sleek lavaliere gobbets.

Leptokurtic trails.
Transient paraesthesia.
Hover—tip and breathe.
Little-leaf linden bower:
Phantom's saunter touch. Lips trace.

Iota feel sparks
Internal cataclysm:
Power constringes.
Frost heave patched in levelled mousse.
Sunsetic lamps. Passion creeps.

Custom Fit

Inclined shoulder's side
Opposite has neckline shaped
Mandibular fang.
Catamount enjoys canine
Tongue thrust short malocclusion.

Rich

Crawling with treacle,
Crust's slightest sapping triggers
Mass extravasate.
La bouchée au chocolat
Coeur coolant de caramel.

Statue in Atrium

Stretching motion as
If removing heavy sword
In sheath along spine.
Feet appear as layered slabs.
Drops: concentric terraced steps.

Pilei with two small,
Distal acorns. Slope paths in
Trumpet petunias.
Artfully valued as if
Adena burial sites.

Vibrato wind swirl
With blending chords: dusting brush
Eskimo kisses.
Static dust swirl in my head
When you face me in my view.

Your stares encourage
Tsunami billow. Stronger
By strategic touch.
Pearlescent, moisturized spread
Dressed anew like japanned tin.

Arms pray in virgulilla formation.
Soft travel on smooth fermata freeze.
Eliminate coarseness:
Abraded by cupping hands.

18

Current

Clear water snow globe.
Opalescent briolettes
In shaken rough sea.
Bright moonlight reveal buoyant
Diamonds: breath from fishbowl bed.

Cold Numb

Graupel beauty from
God's food shaker. Powder spread
Like a swarm of fleas.
Ringing bells: sharp, rapid plucks
From balalaika tickles.

Silken Embrace

Torrid as if bairn
After seeing liquor pour
From a melangeur.
I become tumescent with
Your rinzu kimono touch.

Bond

In noxious grit to
Resist. Travel to calm with
Head paraesthesia.
Enjoying each other in
A great peristalsis pace.

At the Beach

Ambushed by high tide
On dry sands. Passion currents
Fade: breeze…savouring.
Drenched with sweat as if miner's
Soot after laborious day.

Haste Makes Waste

Atramentous and
Taupe bodies run on spot in
Taijiquan fashion.
Energy strong as baby
Birds' hunger after they hatch.

Sweet Arabian Woman

Haldi light thick as
Texas Tea. Attar from a
Rose water fountain.
An Arabian beauty:
Nooshin—strong inside and out.

Pitons in St. Lucia

Woman silhouette
Rest. Chin at Petit apex.
Lush hair—travelled waves.
Thrown back: deep wedge in tree trunk.
What sybaritism brings?

Eyes glisten like blue
Precious stones—Aruba tide.
Search light glow as balm.
Ardour intense: pistons' force
Launched from aircraft carrier.

Medieval Crop

Shakespearean milk
Maid playing theorbo. Her
Pupils face northward.
Astigmatic resistance
To an ophthalmic slit lamp.

Figure fitted dress:
Absence of mildew and grunge.
No vintage age stains.
Consists of a Brassica
Oleracea collage.

Frame protecting hats
On oak horns. Fill congeries
Made with closed-cell foam.
Rotund without corpulence.
Sun rays like dropped jaw seepage.

Danas' Partner

Clear gloss helmet vitrified
With gleam. She is fooled for
Diaphoresis.
By weather or max torque spins,
Winnow will not make it move.

Pellicle immersed
In ochroid sap—dry settled
Around her bone wicks.
One piece bikini Latin
Dress—crystal Fabergé egg.

Houri slowly
Entices: showing off her
Sprayed burka coating.
Destitute of capillum
Except for her scalp and face.

Willoughby's Dea

Bare. Bombolone
Softness. Smooth zabaione…
Enrobed glacé cloak.
Chrome mirror scalp where
Paraffin wax holding strong.

Samba carnival in blues.
In full bloom—tassel and short
Down fluff split panties.
Dreamcatcher burlesque design.
Pom-pom in Cuban motion.

Bra bling pattern:
Infrared light-emitting
Diodes around lens.
Chemiluminescence as
Asiatic lilium solar flare.

Gvantsa

Bent tree silhouette
At dusk. Hair angled: laurel
Wreath for a crown.
Stretched on top Sokolica
Cliff above Dunajec Gorge.

Breasts like wind at sail's
Tightest spread. Find myself in
Magnolia haze.
She struggles to fight off urge…
One comestible in view.

Cowrie

Flannel protection
From sun and deep bitter cold.
Years dust left undone.
Bust: pale softness, silken flock.
Snow drift on the Munro beds.

Beignet sugar when
Runoff dries. Exfoliate
Bracts—tomentose blown.
Trove when finery removed.
Glazed bone china polished curves.

Open balconette
With tight centre isle: seating
Converge to thin hook.
Fortune cookie do not break.
Lumaconi not be stuffed.

Berliner Philharmonie—After Hans Scharoun

Celery fibre-
lingerie lace decorates
Balcony. Dry flake.
Tubers beautifully carved.
Warm glaze on soap rose blossoms.

Vineyard style concert
Hall. Necklace terraces' raked
Tiers. Unusual view.
Full house in the flesh; bag out
Like sails attacked by stiff breeze.

Zantedeschia
Aethiopica: dome spathe
Touched with slow finesse.
Loving harmony. Cleft view
Narrows until hook release.

Dream—After Arthur Braginsky

Strayer wakes by noon
Sun. Head's back—endless strands from
Wavy lava streams.
Astonished as if viewing
An El Capitan fire fall.

Lyssa's Still Life—After Dave Kelley

Boned corset forms vase.
Eastern leaf floral print in
A brocade silver.
Includes satin Indian
Peafowl's iridescent blue.

Slough covering the
Chloasma markings. Ducking
Forms firm chock-a-block.
Acrylic immersion bap-
Tism sans pelagic swim.

Paps behave as plum
And pear still life. Could pass for
Toilet base to rim.
Stable stand with candle pose.
A sluice release in Yichang.

Salekhard

Nger Harp: light of
The dead. A rich vibrancy
Triggers spirit haunt.
An exuberance almost
Psychedelic when sober.

Fluid abstract gaum:
Only light besides distant
Stars this northern realm.
Sand becomes hydrophobic
Paint shaping a fishbowl's floor.

Hauberk—exuviae
From snake during eldritch guard.
Staggering half circles.
Honourable man keeping
Peace retires remaining night.

Dream: Jacaranda
Petals glazed by sturgeon moon's
Crepuscular rays.
A rose laying on rail cap
Of balustrade balcony.

Woman wearing white,
Star bearded iris slip rests
On stone lighthouse pier.

Admiring new indigo
Veil Loutraki sky provides.

Close to equator.
Enjoying shore with his love.
Hypnic jerk awakes.
His concupiscence suffer;
Nympholepsy unfulfilled.

Morena Belle

Cognac cuero belle.
Skin luminiferous dew:
Champagne matte silk blush.
Shayamala soft. Flawless
Warm, filtered, toasty rose flush.

Layered necklace with
Smooth turquoise cushion above
Silver hammered spade.
Holding wine glass. Chain bracelet
Pendulum heart below wrist.

Mooi, toothsome woman:
No cutis anserina
Found on her presence.
American South praline
Sculpture provides needed goose.

Entertained by her
Nymphomania's fluid
Dancing: randy mood.
Peng personality vault
Many piquant memories.

Tavern's Hot Chili Peppers Special

Hippopede: husk on
Medium base sockets. Capped
Kettlebell handle.
Levelled terrain stuffed peppers.
Immaculate landscaping.

Bullhorn narrow wall
Surround trench. Half round coping.
Nordic food plating.
Waterspout spine to my head.
Galvanic laurels: pleasure.

Die-casting

Gulabari soak
After slough. Ripe bloom; sebum
Hold. Rich effulgence.
Livery when bare exposed:
Gehua, sawla, or kala.

Clairsentience: she
Is playing shy. Showing off
Curves with poses.
Spherical, obcordate blades
Fold with sternum space between.

Cowrie shell: mantle
Soft without teeth. Under brush
In desert heat drench.
Convex falcate: red lory
Rostrums' touch form sclera gate.

Perfect Angle to Frame Woods— After Duong Quoc Dinh

Crochet caftan worn.
Bare otherwise like nature.
Finding the best view.
Satyriasis burn as
She reads Anacreontic.

Charlene

Shimmering azure
Satin candle. Cape sleeves as
Loose kite canopy.
Bias cut peignoir with long
V-plunge drapes—'40s trousseau.

Wavy feather flip
With rich ruby shine rests on
Sheena settee chaise.
Double slit middle front skirt.
Scrap flag brings a new pendulosity.

Beyond Reproach

Rosa canina
Seed oil soak encourages
Adamantine youth.
Sweet sabayon/couverture
Cardamom mix without cloy.

Dasha modern
Dress: Ponte De Roma one
Shoulder silhouette.
Odessa Calla lily:
Novel in rich, vehement shine.

Chestnut Waxed

Fuliginous flesh.
Java bean obscure frosting:
Soft peltidium.
Wrinkle-less, tempered chocolate;
Prussian blue charmeuse duvet.

Attracts like moonlight
Hitting samaras glued to
Diamond/sapphire mix.
Moment reminds me: perfect
For Jon Paul book cover art.

Gothic Beauty

Spider mum silken
Weeds on scalp. Limber in prime
Of life. Slithering.
Rolling. Spinning. Dance: turmoil
Energy flow glabrous stem.

Waves top clepsydra:
Curling brim organza hat
Flipping upside down.
Butterfly fruit bowl blooms: spread
Inspired by still-life spout.

Abstruse Tahini
Dream tone. Unvariegated
Complexion her own.
Winter mooli radishes;
Stays plump white hailstones.

Cs, Ps, Ts, and Bs:
Slow creek current pour flowing
Over pallet rocks.
Snap bodily noises when
Drinking. Seductive whispers.

Slider moves to hear
Elements one at a time
Between throats.

Exchange regardless chain or
Open. Stare each other's eyes.

Bubble wrap: each air
Break encourage contraction.
Breath felt on my face.
Smooth finger roll-on: wind tipped
Pollen without touching flesh.

Without drop caffeine,
Fidget as mute Rossini
Coloratura.
Yearn to wedge: rabbit chased dire
Into a warm, deep burrow.

Self Portrait with Muse—After Krzysztof Izdebski-Cruz

Sweet Jasmine quilt with
Leaves and vine squares. May Yellow…
Massless buss on skin.
Above costal cartilages,
Almost complete mitosis.

Chromatin edges
Show off chameleon eyes'
Flexibility.
Triggered round scoop releases
Fill corset like waffle cone.

Nibbled until bare.
Guards for hips' stability.
My own thumbs hover:
Opposing wiper blades on
Periumbilical skin.

Arms above her head
Create diamond silhouette.
Red hair through ring hole:
Smoke from inferno spread by
Santa Ana winds. Wildling.

Astarte—After Jessica Chantry

Desperate grab by
Koi lips. Cast Greek Marble stone:
Samasthiti pose.
Shoulders opener where
Hands interlock above forehead.

Pastoral Symphony's First—After Ralph Vaughan Williams

Tranquillo ending:
Main melody twice in four
Measures. Clandestine lilt.
Violins' four note chords hold
Becomes elegant suspense.

Crystalline spirit.
Glass harp touch on a flush mount's
Satin opal dome.
Stir as breeze whistle moving
Sagisō bloom without chaff.

Musica Serena—After
Pēteris Vasks

Marquess quality.
Rich marchion meets crow's fan tail:
Bay's northerly coast.
Shapes as tigress grabs cub's scruff
Of the neck in standing pose.

One in relevé.
Eyebrows and arms stretched reaching
For high window sill.
Moon shows path. Cannot arrive
To feel one's affection.

Feel sad. Rooting
For deserving soul to have
Blessing to escape.
Helping hand able to make
Desire come true. Happy tears.

Monches to cover on
Ceruse hide anathema
Speed up health unwell.
Ghost beauty in literal
Sense with lead, mercury rot.

Centre lips rouge, while
Rest match foundation, show a

Constant pucker up.
Roquefort becomes disguise as
Argyria—silver null.

Keep in moisture to
Maintain youth by depriving
Sun maximum time.
Idea of perfection:
Stone disguised as stainless steel.

After rest, mend, and
Nourishment: becomes fragrant,
Soften nuzzle feast.
Muslin and dupioni
Trappings removed; camphor cleanse.

Dolcissimo voice.
Petrichor's aeolion.
Grazioso dance.
Irato libido. Growl
Ing ostinato breathing.

Riverboat cradle
Sway sync each legato line;
Stimming to music.
Gentle phrasing with high notes:
Ding from a small hand tea bell.

Compass chisel point
Glides retracing precise path.
Rainbow's slow, tight range.

Seismograph creates sine curves;
Shifting weight at vertices.

Jyotsna kaushiki:
Prabha addax white. Gauri
Aparajita.
Passion's eager: burble from
Huge tidal bore undertow.

I caress her tongue
Repeatedly. Skim soft as
Leopardess takes whelp.
Buccal incubation with
Deep erotic arousal.

Helicopter dust.
Armada fleas swirl:
Silver dragon tails.
Ember attach: sprinkles in
Heat immensely infectious.

Occipital bone
And nape massage as she lays
Facing me on me.
Grace melody soaring high.
Adrenaline go great guns.
Drops in permanent
Hypertropia without
Peal. Undulating.
Tocsins laterals' thumb trails
Feel: full tread on new asphalt.

Even skin tone
Genetic predisposed; gyre
Blossom lapped in dew.
Dove Orchid noodle crammed as
If butterfly lobster tail.

Violin section
Demisemiquavers: rub
Lunaria pod.
Without shred in tempo to
Snake's oscillatory flicks.

Filled aubergine. Dirge,
Limousin drove's perfervid
Pull, inspire congress.
None our volitions oppose.
No will for remedy take.

Defibrillation
Sans convulsion my partial-
Tropefied spirit.
Mill wheel's proxy in blank speed
Like radial arm saw blade.

Headrace overshot
Aim cynosure paddles like
Direct laser beam.
Melody ascends: arch phrase
Galvanic by noria.

Rood-tree roots for strown
Legs as compass traveling.
Span snow angel made.
Limbs have no desire to bend
Except our clenching digits.

53

Tsukiyo

Chinoiserie sky:
Urushi with mother of
Pearl aisle runner gleam.
Fine cloisonné enamel
Vase boldly decorated.

Ivory Floradale
Blooms: beaks tight lipped. Bride white
Hydrangeas: swirl rope.
Hakuun: hand in formal glove.
Convergence make string choked pouch.

Cohesive pyknic
Bodyscape reflects her strong
Turbid latex glow.
Silken fundente becomes
Drarf Yaupons' shiny refuge.

Beauty provides prise
For Duchene sneer becoming
Anjali mudra.
Prim tsukiyama sleeves fain
Cassius larkspur and hold.

Hours later, tension
Gone. Filling painted by clear
Sky dawn. Well and alive.
Turpid mind in paradise:
Massage ends at outdoor spa.

International Rendezvous—After Myles Sullivan

Flowy sheer voile see-
Through backdrop. Sheaths breasts like cupped
Hover from my hands.
Voluptuous blow kisses:
Hard nipples lack garment blind.

Slim, depilated
Monolith. Amaretto
In a concave glass.
Marzipan links tamped and edged
On the top rail balustrade.

One shoulder cut out
Front top. Flesh mini sash through
Neck and underarm.
Her smarmed, narrow tassel cape
Never leaves Cambridge Yard's lip.

I, her newel post,
Feel sacred vibe: pierce swift from
A nocked pin unseen.
Frisson from Pärt's, *Fratres*, springs
Attitude worth cherishing.

Partly cloudy dawn.
My arm at her waist as we
View La Dame de Fer.
A sharp, unintentional
Prick will ruin the moment.

57

Body Art

Carved ovolini
Di bufala—neither herbs
Nor crumbs to grip trace.
Epicurean peignoir.
Vines en masse become silk braids.

Harpist Amongst Ladies in Lavender—After Nigel Hess

Crepuscular ray
Through storm cloud by midnight sun.
Colours mackle sky.
Blue hour other side as if
Evening on Grecian coastline.

Floral fume during
Golden hour. Glissandi in
Me—exquisite swirl.
Continuous melody
Along harp's harmonic arch.

Want to maintain this
Everlasting. She invites
Me with open arms.
Stay to trace many times her
City's analemma curve.

Dolphin Skin—After Mary Phillips

Melt from picture frame
Bumpers spread Kiri mocha
Flow consistency.
Sun mirages on stygian
Flesh lotion maceration.

Seep's glow after souse.
Youthful, glabrate branches show
Salubrious firm.
Oscuro Piloncillo
Cuticle is not too sweet.

Sinuous like breeze
Waving pour—micellar milk
Rich in ceramides.
Gyrate whip: battling rope
Encourage core's serpentine.

Moher cliffs' bestride
After misty fog. Heat from
Interclavicle.
Slightest friction quiver flame
Beacon O'Brien's Tower.

Branaunmore gives full
Attention as I enjoy
Connection and view.
Piano high gloss in sable beauty
Found by the time all is done.

61

Polynesian Beauty—After Enrique Felix

Oil on velvet. Clair-
Obscure soft tonneau cover
With skeleton tree.
Blue moonlight glow as her palms
Clip nape in vajrasana.

Camping pit's flame makes
Caramel sitting rabbit.
Tempered custard shorn.
Side profile lacks coconut
Tail. Fjord betwixt candied eyes.

Asiatic Saturnalia—After Alex Maxim

Shoji Mulberry
Paper like frosted glass. Not
From small tea's steam.
Opening windows present
Traditional Zen garden.

Indefectible
Hematite scalp-coat. Liquid
Glucose acrylic.
Uttana mandukasana:
Parivrtta hasta dab par.

Long black sheer silk gown
Divided into thousands
Of fine noodles hang.
Hiding her bare back smoothed by
Body concealer deluge.

Light spangle display;
Gilded polish on her flesh.
Stretch form shadow track:
Logarithmic graph design.
Premium cushion comfort.

Exposed half naked
By loosened red pyrope
Garnet kimono.
Waiting for lover's return
To bask in her pulchritude.

Defiance or Luminous—After Richard Young

Toffee on cloud white.
Sunrise eyes stranded flower
Taking a bold stand.
Tuberous begonia: sole
Yellow on Bermuda grass sea.

Pineapple squiggles…
Ramen noodles fall streaked by
Branded balayage.
Fool for tough bromelain; wave
Space shape spike tiles' home.

Honey balsamic
Marinade or brown sugar
Vinaigrette topping.
Obfuscate: circumfuse like
Fudge torrent edged on cookie.

Interference in
My head: intoxicated
Or low blood sugar.
Numb as body fights ragweed
Bothering my sinuses.

French horn's moving cue:
Eidolon enthralled refrain.

Then, I walk circles.
Lost track time it took before
Notice failure to free mind.

Garden enchanted;
Hiding our intimacy
From entire public.
Romantic concealment spell
Conjured by nature and love.

Hay bales' bond onto
Granary. Sleek dark amber
Agave complexion.
Storage in bunker ready
For launch at moment's notice.

Charged flow: viewing rough
Buffaloes' career within
Yards of taken path.
Voided with aid from bruit and
Finger licks while limbs in cinch.

Music of the Body—After Ruslan Bolgov

Swivel facing bass
Clef keys. Backless gown's halter
V-neck strings untied.
Nineteen momme charmeuse silk drapes
To the floor as she performs.

Clavicles necklace
Still rests. Plumber's crack intend
Not to be covered.
Vertical elliptic Booth
Lemniscate behind cleavage.

Under the Cover—After Anna Ewa (Hannah) Miarszynska

Wevet white uncracked
Eggshell; body's base gesso.
Wrapped towel on her waist:
Moist, silken magnesium
Aluminium silicate.

Except eye lashes
And brows and crown with sprouted
Spiral curls. Wrap loose:
Uncovers two mirroring
Breaking waves before plunging.

Mehndi

Henna designs faux
Lace lingerie; webbing pall
Shrouds her bare body.
Spice grinder's khandsari bath…
Muscavado candlelight.

Cadillac fins with
Dodge Charger circles during
New Raqs Sharqi show.
These tail light eyes see dancer's
Bubble-less egg custard bulk.

Guarded cover for
Sinhala Fayanna with
Coins' mesmerized hiss.
Bedlah hardwear highlighted
By balconette pettinice.

Camels, vaksh snaps, and
Deep back bend: expectorants
For fountain spitter…
Cherubim as sculpted stone.
The wedding will soon take place.

Fire Glow—After Stephen Pearson

Obscure sky except
Hints from moonlight blue disguised
As chalk foundation.
Gold olive monochrome for
Candles' light keeps body warm.

Shiny velvet. Smooth
Nap. Butterfly emerges
From her chrysalis.
Marinade with tarconite.
Full volume mash after sparge.

Archaic Lie Supine—After Antigoni Tziora's, *Teressa II*

Shoulder opener
Parvatasana. Oxters'
Cleavage—squeaky slides.
Limbs sprawl; splayed for pressure rise
Infinitesimally.

Sautéed bust lids off
Centred as if mouth at chin
Muscles' highest push.
Arched back hangs over bed edge.
Ride wave crest head first to shore.

Moon in Colours—After Brenda Paige

Had to move things for
House repairs. Took break looking
Through one storage box.
Found with rested dust remains
Of ugly Christmas outfit.

Sole section survived
After dog got tangled then
Canine teeth broke free…
After few years great cooking
And company memories.

Strawberry batch of
Holiday bulbs dangle while
Wrapped on sweater arms.
Fuzzy matching socks with glass
Substitutions for sleigh bells.

Scarf yarn travel in
Liquorice putty straight rows
With yellow band stripes.
My phone tied on pocket-less,
Vertical striped pencil skirt.

Wore only once a
Top that was heavy, tight, and

Made my neck itchy:
Red, ribbed design, fine knit, long
Sleeve turtleneck pullover.

Toddler cries when told
To take a nap then asleep
Near the natural pine:
About ten minutes after
While looking at ornaments.

Zooming in and out
Viewing mirrored baubles. In
Awe of glass angels.
Ceramic houses with false
Candlelight on cotton snow.

A Fauvism art
Representation of my
Time having nickname.
Known by family and friends
As Electric Reindeer elf.

Discs and Bracelet—After Johan Swanepoel

Overlapping discs
Link chain choker with bar striped
Grater cuff bracelet.
Sophisticated posh pose;
Mannequin torso.

Chaste, unbromidic
Nangi. Damenakt flesh in
Black and white photo:
Unbruised, satin finish with
Deep, bold stainless-steel smoothness.

Thick caoutchouc feuille.
Unrolled tuxedo truffle
Mousse foundation tread.
Morn: Matsyasana sit. Skin:
Coffee and milk monochrome.

Doves Look After Her—After Natali Zaboltskaya

Long tongue drape places
Woman in supine as if
From eagle toe lift.
Copper coils without candle-
Light. Stage crew opposite side.

Doves' Valentine's Day.
Providing romance spirit
For lover she waits.
Roller coaster ride foreplay…
Gentle blow trace without slot.

Internal Downpour—After Kostiantyn Shyptia's, *Rain*

Finger massage on
Bead button areas with-
Out divot pressure.
Asynchronous drizzle spring
Cloudburst drops from under skin.

Cari—After Casey Yoshida

Wet Smetana spread.
Filled, beautiful woman mould
Frees gulab jamun.
Rasgulla: immersed meetha
Polish in every tongue touch.

White, off-the-shoulder
Dress dipped as well in pond bed
Sans colour runoff.
Sea through experience but
Not quite totally limpid.

Rescued her; after
She bathed and dried, we snuggled
To keep body warm.
Chattering teeth she suffers
No more. Rest foreheads tangent.

White Orchid, Jasmine,
Santalol: warm vanilla
Comfort in the air.
Missord one shoulder cut out…
Flesh cream dariya exposed.

Second Symphony Chorus—After Gustav Mahler

Synchronized trembles
Murmur: idling engines'
Directionless pit.
Fears' precursor shocks where it's
Undetermined soul at threat.

Roaring carbines far
Away via winter howl
And airliner launch.
Autumn all year. Antique glazed
Gargoulette becomes dust wad.

Baily's bead as if
Air continuously bonds
With luciferin.
This light is not coming from
Firefly; no man-made source seen.

Red bronze pearl mica
Microns thick. Matte cover like
Urethane sculpture.
Tonic preserve with neither
Glitter nor swirl marmalade.

Astounding beauty
Sitting with her oboe. Skin

Basting without glow…
Til microdermabrasions'
Windsor tan ceramic glaze.

Bold majolica:
Smooth Rookwood terracotta
Orcio puglia.
Dark umber glaze: halo shine
After rich jocheong's salt bath.

No zante currant
Found in treacle sea. Wave not
From stirred wind or tow.
Settled zabaglione
Fill when casing mould undone.

No spit roasting is
Necessary to even.
Spastic reach: from my
Twenty digits not. Her breeze
Brings arrector pili chill.

Dawn swells: birds in roll
Aggravated stalls with tight
Corkscrew rotations.
Pirouettes up the sky while
Sycamore seeds' downward yaw.

Metal Guppies

Not talking about
Cute people tempting me to
Rub their facial cheeks.
Not children with sippy cups.
Not about chubby people.

Not about liking
Hardrock music. Neither man
Nor cartoons involved.
Super, Pregnant, and Mini:
NASA has them—they can fly.

Female Attila

Posing strength as if
Prepared for war. Hunger found
After long slumber.
Thrived impulse from a walrus
And polar bear rivalry.

Fresh, renewed cover.
Blood rushing like lava paths
Encouraging grunts.
Crawl like panther until she
Faces me top my body.

Two fluid drops not
Able to break free. Ripened
Spheres connect flat slope.
Kissing by drawing inkless,
Light circles onto my chest.

Her territory
Marked. Fingertips on the hips;
Butter glaze on rolls.
Soft, satin cases. Floral
Fruit entice savouring flood.

Terrain on my face.
Mollified with her protein
Bar perimeter.
Lustful music. Sensual
Toughness by lasting wrestle.

82

Shirley

Mandolin of the
East. Clean, crisp voice becomes charmed
Massage to the mind.
Harp with bridges beside heart.
Medieval sublime beauty.

Blackbeard

Quiet, takes his time.
Balancing a phone on his
Head without moving…
When facing him. Loves being
Held like baby on shoulder.

Rather people stare
Than watch television. Will
Sit on toilet seat-
Or sink until shower done.
Basket hide when laundry done.

Lay beside you with
Paw on your arm or face like
Finding "Where's Waldo?"
See living room from upstairs
Through narrow door and wall edge.

Too cute!!!!

Omi—After Abdiel Jacobsen

Wiggly rope; sustain
Ripples. Sinuous: moving
Thick falls—ribbon folds.
Zheemoo board keeps ball on front
Torso while traveling through.

Rolls: flexure funnel
Clouds. Caterpillar stuck in
Wrap while freeing self.
Frustrated. Is there hope in
Future for freedom to reign?

Wax bolus loosen.
Stretch in sun's path from jungle
Foliage blanket break.
Listen to crepitation
And stridulation ensembles.

Bling Flurries

Sweat; glitter fall from
Christmas card shaken. Same edge
Sapphire, velvet gown.
Finer than salt before melt.
Not perspiration—for dance.

Edamame

Samara pouch with
Triplet gems tucked tight. Beanie
Propeller muscles.
Eichel's heavier end: slight
Apply flashes sharp response.

Shrimp's soy diet. Leech
Fills after plum rain. Seaplane
Float escapes capped nose.
Crus becomes wing side arch flapped
Full span for softer landing.

Flytrap captures slug
Trespassing farmland. Kunai
Knife: disguised moustache.
Training blade provides skaters'
Protection. Sown spiracles.

Schrzart Und Innig—After Gustav Mahler

Puffed fog spread sun ray
Blinds developing the sky's
Astigmatism.
Jalousie opens: present
Experience short man's twig.

Morning's clarified
Samneh flood autumn leaves from
Thick, untilled acres.
Comb's labourers have citrine
Beyond space capacity.

Bunjingi triggers
Memory etched on matte fine
Art bamboo paper.
Sepia ink wash; olive
Green bistre atmosphere.

Apotheosis
In musealized pose. Stretched a-
Nuvittasana.
Aperitive inspires numb;
Nerves' presto celesta swarm.

Komorebi like
Borehole after lassoing

Stalagmite in cave.
Piquant body soufflé bold
Solid none my fell has felt.

Has demonstrated
Éclat's best. Splendid hauteur
Without arrogance.
Too restrained for condition.
Love to show solicitude.

Awning stripped—raindrops'
Targets not yet fathomed to
Fancy preference.
Entities manifest—bare
Thoughts not descried hitherto.

Mountain Gum treated
In pedi scrub gel: buffed off
All of the shedding.
Recovered by being doused
With baking soda shower.

Wasp galls burgeon on
Bark by zephyr snap. Pimply
Comes temporary:
Fall in unison compared
To boil flatten to simmer.

Curved neck busts wishbone
Connected. Graduated
Rivières round trim.

Twin large cabochons of sard
Carnelian untraversed.

Kvell while her chortle
Makes maiden voyage beating
On my myringas.
Contralto stream without pulp;
Brings comfort as chrism squab.

Down texture none has
Indulged. High tremolo in
Dramatic suspense.
Fountainhead springs sans my
Reaction sent from taste buds.

Verge still as chess piece.
Noble posture facing God's
Panorama cleanse.
Waft from ledge provided an
Inviting path to adit.

Insect bands request
Attention with fervour from
Stadium seating.
Wings ribbing on button spot
As if trombones' tight, fast slides.
Lithe scourges distend
Upward—spinning whirligigs.
Iron Jaw acrobats:
Zest with neither cable nor
String in prodigious joy.

Side-straddle hop spread:
Pulling done invisible
Without punishment.
Set up neither quartering
Nor for a crucifixion.

                    91

Air of lachrymose
Grace. Moment's pause—evanesce
To or from darkness.
Josef Hoffmann art comes to
Mind: Aus dem Brünhildenstein.

Sirius

Crystal flashes spread
High pitched whistle. Seraphim
Wings needed for eyes.
Melodies with woman voice
Staves. Flickering candle flare.

Vibraphone single
Note strike with carrying depth.
Bouncy wobble spring.
Borborygmi tracked in di-
Pyramid prismatic.

Verrillon whir. A
Trombone's mute, lip, or slide trill.
Atmosphere refracts.
Lighted toggle switch when off;
Express oneself in Morse code.

Air cycling in
Womb. Recumbent trike stuck
Trying to escape.
Orion's belt virgule points
Down to changing glow fibre.

Enamorada—After
Jesus Helguera

Diosa chaplet
Snug with dark, rich curls along
Pappus cloud highlights.
Mystic power's slow sprouting;
Urlicht's diamond ring effect.

Rising during a
Renascence not wholly awake
In comforted mind.
Wet, smooth, mirror reflective
Corrective covering glow.

Xtabentun redolence
Surround ceiba tree. Idi-
Osyneratic way:
Catch attention short my trust
For this frumusete zeita.

Derecho's thunder,
Along skyline approaching,
Provides warning vibe.
Her arms unrolled relieved for
Winter chill recovery.

Almost creating
Portrait collar neckline. Wrapped

Ends make draped cap sleeves.
Valance waterfalls hang top
Notched over bust hunches.

Reminds which John Keats
Expressed. I am ensorcelled
As she goes away.
However, sharpened thorns seen
Kept me at bay. Saved my life.

Water Dancer—After
Anna Miller

Melanin pay on
Gold minion sea. Bhavai dance
With water pitcher.
Flame substituted by drops
For great velocity shifts.

Hidrosis flow mix:
Globe chandelier sparingly
Disperse seed aigrettes.
Unseen alveolate for
Cutaneous respiring.

Performing in a
Blending silk skirt and necklace
Filled with cowrie beads.
Service plate cover domes topped
Ornate ring-less finials.

Cuarta position…
Half naked bailaora
Without tilted head.
Epilated soft serve slide
Along Alhambra stonework.

Pierné Opus Nine

Daedal workings on
Gypsum. Champagne flutes: stems hold
Kneecap vertices.
Friction breath on internal
Reflections' cosseted trails.

Maquillage frosted
Clad on chiffon. Clench crisp as
Austenitic steel:
Vanadium blend on golf
Driver crown's contour.

Fulgid, nitid peel
In rutilant light. Supple.
Achenes spring like chills.
Dendrite fractals on windshield
Cannot scrape off one fell swoop.

Circle arc compass
Run my pendulum lips like
Typewriter platen.
Savour cob without maize out.
Bulge radius' slow scribble.

Intra 5 for Orchestra—After Max Richter

Feeding from contact
Repetitions. Fluttering
Wrestle with tillers.
Sensitive, passionate tines.
Ice confection's light suction.

Inflatable tube
Dance. Furtherance stifles flex.
Marionettist…
Tongue takes invisible string.
Silo without chassis need.

Impermanence; hence,
Melodies repeat.
Layering so not to leave.
Trigger soul too movingly
Emote. Receive second wind.

Cocooned by entire
Body embrace: crumpled not.
Flurries sugar hood.
Crutch above my lap acting
As still frame humpback breaching.

Amenity grows
Providing voice to bond: we're
Always together.
Keen moan with tears. Gentle touch
As if sleek and frangible.

Photographic Essay

Cyan monochrome.
Vanilla, geranium,
Rosewood, and ylang-ylang.
Haze is not detrimental
To her flexure entices.

Hands camber along
Crooks. Great pains taken as if
Tapioca pearls.
Velvety Masonite hue
Peep out from avocados.

Lack crinosity
Below eyes. Yogini at
Engevika shore.
Philippine Gold complexion:
Limber richness to the core.

Volumetric light
Grabs yellow ranunculus.
Sheaves fondle her flesh.
Felt in fug before relief;
Noticed on golf's bent grass green.

A ballerina
Arabesque releases bird
Flock and butterflies.

Down floating cradles; bonfire
Ember adumbrations fly.

Illusion like pic
Of friend finger holding the
Tower of Pisa.
Tattoo something pretty to
Complement scattered birthmarks.

Priapic starling
Formation. Subtle as search
For moon libration.
Long voyage to rice water
Coated kurokami strands.

Simulacrum of
Libra's crave for balance while
In sculling synced glide.
Sound made after trying to
Remember—comes sudden spray.

Peanφttsmφr dusk
Neither cloud nor Maui's Ropes.
Gas rotunda bold.
Ships without Jacobs Ladders
Add to synapse library.
Mali garnet flame
Bloom. Anti-crepuscular
Leaves; arrows centred.
Grace pose brings to mind linens
Held peg tipped with effete blows.

Gridding tape inks the
Connections of hunter
Asterisms' dots:
Cobweb lingerie design
Lack covering between silk.

Exuberance when
Presented bare Ambon: stretched,
Plumb embouchure.
Lioness Rampant faces
Me; Sheffer Stroke peak awakes.

Illimité bike
Of peas emerge on her brawn
Detecting my lips.
Tuberose perfume; act when
Door opens after shower.

Spumante fill through
Spinal cord. Glitter swirls in
Crystal figurine.
Tongue, reins: firm streamer ends on
Baton sustain cyclone winds.

Doyen with unfurled
Cudgel becomes maestra of
Musical duet.
Feel tight squint series between
Her soft pommesgabel stanchions.

Noshing's gnarled voice. Veers
Backward while astride, laying,
Or lean onto wall.
Bathe sprawled without garment spoor:
String nor circumbendibus.

Perfectly postured
Zafus. Cerulean seines
Fill without trawl boat.
For assist, gives me full throw
Into campanulate sea.

Galvanizing spurt
From kinuskikastike
Disembogued recent.
Settled like galvanized iron.
Fingers skimmed in aquaplane.

Tahini dressing
With one sesame freckle.
Brigadeiro plain.
Cloudless mocha hada. My
Touch cause hoarfrost to assail.

Rout in ceiling trap
Preventing total retreat.
Fish' buoyant eggs freeze.
Horde like ants unable to
Eat their way out to freedom.

Time trial helmets
In waxed alopecia.
Raised budino nap.
Fresh swamp in tempera lick.
Cranberry Lingerie Bridge.

My palms bowl on half
Pipe lanes under her shoulders.
Fresh bare, open cuffs.
Glossal wrestle fuel hoist:
Rope taut includes one end free.

Au bade

Solar lentigo
In curvesa sharp hold. Trails
Of bobbin lace found.
Given by Sol's light as a
Souvenir for years' service.

Other flesh with beams
Give beauty thick junket froth.
Smooth by cast calfskin.
Liquid latex disguise as
Sateen flat sheets on mattress.

Pastilles embraced.
Opaque warm, incandescent
Chest vanity sconce.
Candelabra globes' poise like
Pulpous Hitohada gel.

Intimate boardwalk:
Netting twin falcate drops. Strap
On marsh. Maebari…
Pectin rich plum. Kawaii
Mochi silk wrapped by high fork.

Russet alcorza
Slide. Lustrate in Kobicha
Tea. Bulwark from age.

Architectural neckline:
Symmetric wind sail winged cups.

Arched silhouette walls
With perforated designs.
Guard for firm maintain.
Parapetto's luxury
Prevents escape body mould.

Fishbone V neck crop
Top corset. Wide square neckline
Romantic gothic.
Eighteenth century empire
Bustier regency stays.

I hone for you. Your
Crowing, roister or soft, in
My meditation.
Yelp triggers auralism
Leading to mutual whoop.

My touch and taste in
Overwhelming hanker for
Spring's settled top-dress;
On bride's bare as I performed
Its circumnavigation.
She presented a
Fashion show. Skirt slits through front
At both thighs' centres.
Under bust boned: scoop neckline
With halter straps cinched at nape.

Exfoliated
Skin sans fingernails. Better
While in bathing wet.
Unlike remove cured latex
Ink from tickets or gift cards.

Massive strength takes me
While gourmandizing sweetness
Of her dishabille.
Midriff seiches flow with buoyant
Button along lake's skyline.

Pear slice fang tip each
Platito cup, thick support
Beyond nipples' edge.
Soigné gown on castana
Mannequin. Morenas dote.

Her only request
For vesture is button-less
Powdered clove soutane.
Criollo succolade spread
Inundated her figure.

No smoked harissa
Kreupelhout hedge below her
Mane crown's bottom edge.
Her stagnant melachroiní
Tributaries now divulged.

Mewed up as if a
Dunked cantucci. A thatch sea
Without growth above.
Unabridged reedmace catkin
Limbs. Non-cacophony voice.

La Chair de Poule

White raceme pair: soft
Farmer's Dendrobium guard
In full bloom ambit.
Anther cap fool for nestling's
Beak for gaping protrusion.

Sepals and petals
Become stretched doves' wings. Column
Faces hide in track.
Fallen dominos—ribbon
Spread card deck except apex.

Peep out during slight
Breath like goose-pimples, phono
Graph horn capped cannons.
Loaded in warship—wait for
Ambush at captain's command.

Victoria Falls'
Feely bows. Manubrium
Chasm his face rests.
Sink like a silk, puff mattress.
Lips trail mountain back on top.

Exposed pre-hatched spawn
From giant semelparous
Dofleini tight net.

Hectocotylus touch brings
Aciniform explosion.

Temporary spume
Captured top root beer ocean.
Awakening push:
Without cumulonimbus
Flammagenitus detach.

Whippet Beauty

Ghost strands: cataract
Draped till roll up to see through
Window's overview.
Elysian fields being
Blocked by white domatera.

Arcady's dawn: mixed
Buttered Maca foundation
When beams scan prim hedge.
Sharks enthralled by cay's idyll
Scent hale turtles uneaten.

Rejoice in numen's
Aesthetic presence. Blessings
From great tutelar.
Sashay knuckle-crawling swag
Show territory master.

Clothing consists of
Solely bikini suds with
Floral scent refresh.
Consummate starkness to show
Slick adroitness for the touch.

Vanilla lather:
Wet broderie anglaise just
Above bath water.

Antiseptic perfection
Newly released from bandbox.

An omnipresent
Perspective as a fly views
From spot not disturbed:
Through large gap of door and jamb
Between tenon and mortise.

Mugent and anise
Spread along peristyle while
Divan placed centre.
Shine when inuksuk sanded
Like polished ebony plates.

Halter neck criss-cross
Cut out crop cami top. Wave
Triangle centred:
Between her inner-side breasts
Pretend to be flipped vestette.

Vantablack bottle
Film protecting her essence
Premier quality.
Tsampurado: tabliya
Melt for merienda joy.
Arrayed herself in
Sable cream adorning flesh
Like hollowed figure.
Ameliorate any
Roughness sign so to devour.

Baste: bathed from kiln all
Drippings trapped. Delectable
For all my senses.
Cordial high: nipples puffed as
If invertase-centered fill.

Unctuous without
Residue: demitasse slide.
Bracken lanolin.
Coulis showing off: sidle
Required track hiatus free.

Slump to the side as
If on armrest. Haute model
Pose her own bare curves.
Smooth dashboard lamina for touch.
Tender shuck not to remove.

Buried sleughs; finger
Trails not noticed. Paraffin
Silken marinade.
Inverted dimples: shields in
Testudo with pleasure moans.

Her breaths spring aim my
Skin's shower jet nozzle bites
With pull upright hairs.
Perfume reminds—blackberry
Brandy on Tunnock's teacakes.

Hibiscus tea waves:
Sorrel gelatine becomes
Roasted beet sauce slice.
Boisette moins rough leather feel.
Hair rich in acajou shades.

My head feels during
Sauvium: massage like calf
Fed on mother's teet.
Wallaman Falls in grail for
Parishioners' souls strengthen.

Mutual frottage
In close bachata hold: frames
Embracing instead.
Caressing bolero swoop.
Foxtrot with right ribs' axis.

Okusoma on
Our mutual right legs. Belt
Out energy zest.
Wire sponge topiary band
Pointing towards a tunnel.

Chirp tremolo flit
From fife. Esca roams: firefly
Moves without traipsing.
Humpback anglerfish lure—tyke
Approaches apocrine scent.

Song from touch singing
Bowl rim like gentle rub on
Rubber jar gripper.
Perputial massage on cap
Balanus soda bottle.

Keeping afloat in
Full osunic spirit with
Spiral distortion.
Rowing to closest river
Coast with leaking wood pirogue.

Maestra leads gripping
Jazz baton bulb—edge tipping
With introitus.
Chiropsia without hands.
Palpation non-medical.

Her talisman soul;
An internal periapt.
Deep intelligence:
Invisible bindi form-
Ing special phylactery.

Do not want to be
Numb everything beyond my
Epidermal sphere.
Petting bitumen: pleasure
By mutual satisfy.

Torneira at wax
Maximum. Caralho looms
Enjoying presence.
Nodding every contraction;
Occiput hits tummy wall.

Canorous flow is
Beyond ravishing. Bubbles
Distorted avoiding bursts.
Moob-bang for polyestrous
Adventures to be desired.

Lacrymae escape
Palpebrae. Resonating
Quiver brings relief.
Subwoofers vehemently move:
Grace without distortion made.

Only with consent
She gives for this beautiful,
Moving escapade.
Lovely cheer desired—not for
Sadeian puissance seize.

Limerence fulfilled
By volupté jouissance.
Imbibe gamma burst.
Sweat torrent: desiccation
Until excess drips removed.

Prurient spirit
Thrust: mesmerizing onrush.
Gaderffii reversed.
Cling nail marks: gratifying
Vestige from unknown now known.

Jessye of Augusta—In Honor of the Late Jessye Norman

Invisible rapid falls
Free from heavy stems and rocks.
A consummate sound:
Dulcet and mellifluous.
Values beauty old and new.

Fog conceals the sky's
Ephelides. Wanting campground
At Burleigh's river…
Expressing in deep, rich waves.
Spirit inspired young in awe.

Moth orchid hybrid…
Dedicate in her honour.
Seed parent: crossbreed
Allegria and Auteuil.
Pollen parent: Tetelrath.

At sunset for time
On Earth. *September*: *morning…*
While going to sleep.
Memories *spring* emotions.
Be at peace amongst angels.

Amelia Or Maria—After Giuseppe Verdi's, Simon Boccanegra

White shift underneath
Wearing pearl raindrop earrings.
Purple mantelet.
Princess line cotehardie:
Oxford blue velvet square neckline.

Winged behind ears and
Waves further down as a ripe
Wheat field at sunset.
A forest edge diadem:
Landscaping above forehead.

Bright, firm limacon
Kissing night skyline. Tangent
Harbour ends—sea midst.
View inspires observation:
Lovers' amplesso first time.

Humbled; ascetic
Modesty allows blessing
To love. Failed kidnap.
Pray amongst citizenry's
Fierce acrimony for peace.

Dance: Ten, Looks: Three—After Marvin Hamlisch

Mkhedruli Oni,
Lao Fo Sung, Kannada Ba,
Arabian Seen:
Sans Schnabel poulaines. Lanna
Ka, Sankethi Ha stemless.

Devanagari
La escapes Hebrew daleth.
Tulu Tha dual:
Off rail-carriage. Lek Hora
Seven lost her own sabre.

Lambadi Ja torn
From tilde. Tibetan Ya.
Monocular Glyph…
Geminate not to see through.
Nepali Gha: bracket fell.

Pirouette

Front bonnet hood badge.
Mazda arabesque en pointe.
Daihatsu stretch forms-
Catch-foot camel. Loose emblem's
Hypermobile attitude.

Will not meet deadline
For a telegraph flower
Delivery by…
Making weeks' topspin like golf
Ball on tee screw into ground.

Vorspiel and Salvation—After Richard Wagner's, Parsifal

Giant bubbles: gnats
Lower from ocean's ceiling.
Dulce reap's deep swallows.
Jam shake—velutinids in
mesopelagic slag lamp.

Slow undercurrent.
Prime Gunnera leaves behave
As pistons warming…
Product line. Undulating
Arms without ecdysiast.

August seamounts by
Earth's faults and volcanic weld.
Highfalutin ridge:
Untouched; not reachable by
Bare ensemble strongest men.

Maestro repeats wrap…
Uncoiling helical spring.
Elbows growing space:
Avidly avoids injure.
Layering to form cocoon.

Piccolo quiver chirps
From triple star. Ghost fountain's

Yumbilia form.
Moth's followspot strikes mocked by
Hysterical paroxysm.

Mountain lion's loud ouch
Roars in crystalline tone. A
Melody effect:
Motion from cetacean flukes
Fit along single word, 'Gral'.

Canon perpetuus:
Circle of fifths with gear change
Different chorus joins.
Light's swell as doves manoeuvre
With pixie dust on contrails.

Sharp doubt octopus
Provides when making ambush
Leap to capture prey.
Ribbing male crickets. Drag from
Full speed race cars without sound.

Plagal Cadence.

Nehmet Hin Meinen Leib—After Richard Wagner

Quake on submarine
Canyon. Hear undercurrent's
Turbidity wash:
Snarls from dramatic tiger
Streak in dark Byzantium.

Throat quaffing: piston
In constant motion. Bubble
Pockets vacillate.
Drone's descent to abyssal plain.
Seen no more by human eye.

Miaul glissandi…
Tilde in periodic
Dynamics. Rhythm:
Mocking rotation beacon.
Dolphin super pod leaping.

Fiend weight bearing with
Authigenic pulvil. All
Quicksand in contuse.
Cleansing light thrusts downward as
Haze stripes fall multiple folds.

Provides firm, steady
Hold stopping victim's hobbling
Crawl on laced trauma.
Spirit freed with ghostly flag.
Sanitized by heaven glaze.

Sarcophagus

Fondant death mask: white
Chocolate perpetuate
Slab disguise for crypt.
Dressing superior to
All Medusa eyes' designs.

Cast marble's gorgeous
Tintoretto detail. A
Polished chacolong:
Create spiral orb web for
Lattice chain mail shirt and coif.

King piece surrenders
Laying down on chessboard. Prays
Without a lace shroud.
Resin paralysis with
Alabaster and limestone.

Invisible beam
From nebula with Cat's Eye's
Focus on Queen's heart.
Swelling dense clear quartz spread. Sense
Divine channelling on soul.

A master healer's
Tributaries flood her cheeks…
Mountain snowmelt surge.

Aching mourn chills nucha path.
Beads' javelins buoy in place.

Pentelic neighbour
With halo gold stands facing
Carrera's beauty.
Permanent open eyes till
Black yeast biofilm surround.

Part of a Year—After Owen Francis Hand's, Home of The Whale

Barge shipping coal for
Heating. Soot moved off; hard to
Come clean. Touch and breath:
Leavening agents for her
Pleasure with grass seed spacing.

Catholically filled
By toriadhean builen. Swell
Of spotted deòir.
Roux flesh in envermeiled gold.
Fìor: wincing without pain.

Gantin on me as
Her knees on paillasse. Uchdan's
Cìoch-shlugain hang.
Growth narrow boat loom in fog.
Arms in transept exposure.

Glossal entwine, with
Current and against grain, flow
Adagio pace.
Then, fast as rabbit scribble
To remove pediculus.

Burnet rose presence
Intoxicates. Focus on
Hip fastigia.
Ripen berries intended
Not for teeth's grave detachment.

Apse smiles at me as
I make light, lip-pinch steps through
Her cìochan nave.
Slithering on broillichean
Parapets how ants infest.

Time too precious to
Be together for torment's
Rage to demist glass.
Fastigium behaviour
Without sickness to be cured.

Bond strongest ever.
Temporary lassitude.
Holiday has passed.
My job's requirements amongst:
Leave my love, return to sea.

Roundabout's Simplicity—After Dave Kelley

Cobalt blue flute stands.
Pudendum cloth splits sandfall's
Fine, white rice sprinkles.
Projector's laser beams move:
Fight targets when aim one spot.

Cafu vase base with
Three tier one-sheeted hyper-
Boloids. Hurricane:
Candleholder of flared glass;
A wavy pillar lantern.

Slow slide on cambered,
Haloed moon skin. Finger trace
Groove less meander.
Silken tofu chilled. I feel
Neither flakes nor switch fibres.

Recorder's tone holes:
Another amplifier
Back side intended.
Double hole dimple; there are
Some that are blocked by design.

Couple of them for
Sweet nothings. Window nostril

Has cartilage split.
Few can be used to express…
Held in place or wavering.

Mermaid femme fatale:
Fin corrugated pear wrapped.
Phial bottom open.
Head's asteroid star: flame becomes
Double Hershey's Kiss far back.

White Fresnel spot. A
Cyclorama backdrop from
Filtered luminaire.
Black bars like letterboxing
With figure centered out screen.

Pause inspires silent
Melody: music only
From my mind. Presence:
How soft, smooth, lovely just short
Of cloy. Light bold match fresh paint.

Nitid, chatoyant
Double face satin ribbon.
Chrysoberyl eye:
Cabochon gemstone pupil…
Skin where dress cannot connect.

Pareidolia

Hyaluronan
Cells' corpulence a thousand
Times. Fenugreek gum:
Thickening such glazed finish forms
With whisked pumpkin's high sheen.

Mimicked: Cassia
Angustifolia seed
Polysaccharide.
Shiso, Perilla extract,
Alexandrian Senna.

Runge's roulade thew…
Argillaceous spread. Brackets
Hair: tassel tieback.
Retinol plumps firm skin. Levelled
Kaymak: syllabub dew's sleek.

Coulis without lumps;
Sugar treat not surfeit.
Poi tails' passion flames.
Spearmint candy canes become
Pillar candles without wick.

Adrenaline swirl:
Throw full weight into spinning
Qilumitautit.
Her salmon gum bark shredded.
No lack munificent touch.

Snake Knot

Webworms and Eastern
Tent Caterpillars infest.
Stress-free braids: cane rows.
Cornrows' tousled tops. Fuzzy
Two-strand twist dreadlock fingers.

Serpents freeze reaching
To feel for warmth from eyebeams
Like rack with hairspray.
Manchineel tree branches: horns
Run amok. Julienne cut.

Defoliate like
Napalm. Vulnerable as
Unstitched bullet hole.
Risking disease or death
If tree not cared properly.

Bevy Float of Dancers

Rose flamboise shine on
Wall from stage PAR Can light as
Antisolar rays.
Cinematic silhouette
Develops dark purple hue.

Animatronics'
Solid up and down without
Anything quaking.
Performance loops like using
Wooden plunger butter churn.

Bolero's wide leg
Stride. Body ripple waves. Feet
Without relevé.
Expressing their venery.
Gliding without falling on ice.

Cars' wrap guards released.
Catching as bodice plastron.
Factory ordered:
Fine berries chutney varnish.
Prime on choux profiterole.

Eye candy angles.
Giza necropolis dance
Swooping melody.

Kanjivaram pattu sacks
When I barely touch bodies.

Metallic waters.
Tanzanite indigo sleek:
Interlagos' fleek.
Ramekins flip bavarois.
No prediction for sunder.

Titian hair with
Brine-cured stems' Kalamata
Aceituna shine.
Rufescent, gules, cochineal,
Claret lips: new tints display.

Chiffon cape and front
Drape—champagne flute funnelling
Between ilia.
Through tieback band without side
Straps to still their silhouettes.

Pelvic bone cleavage.
Double slit front Grecian gowns.
Connect at shoulders...
As if pinned on clothes line on
Same pins at their widest sides.
Hourglass frozen in
Time. Double easel stands with
Canvas smocks sans shelves.
Smooth, adust, euprous, demi-
Glacé skin with a dank sheen.

Smooth seep from asphalt
Volcano on sea floor. Bar
Buoyancy cresting:
Ocean surface thick cape touch
Ing troposphere's bottom edge.

Scottish Tipsy Laird:
Carob blancmange on trifle
Just moments before:
Desire resistance collapse
For slight fingerprint sample.

Dry spray clear finish:
Abstergent freshens after
Cutting and buffing.
Detritus invisible.
Resilient all over.

Nose missing nares on
Vertex pitchfork trails in folds
Nasolabial.
Effleurage—use my gentle,
Padded tips encircling.

Quill web: slow sweat beads
Roll down her contours. Apex
Resonance quaver.
Follow colour spectrum slides…
Prism tiny glint glory.

Gel film's pavonine:
Goniochromism from
Mallard duck's plumage.
Hygge: friable finger
Draw on tengujo intact.

In a Landscape—After John Cage

Fragrance: genie bare
Fully open from keystone
Cinnamon bottle.
Teimhneach screen caliginous
As well as fuliginous.

Collagen rich with
Mediterranean made
Glycerone soaked in.
Behaving without meaning
For close. Air-conditioned chill.

Harp string standing on
Each goose-pimple. Warming whir
Pianissimo.
Touch light as breeze through my lips.
Music from your keening throat.

Matka—After Olga Ziemska

Yoseki—wooden
Mosaic sculpture. Bough pile.
Arboreal art.
Vector mapping wind flutter.
Not a human porcupine.

Think passage bulwark
Found at ocean cliff zenith.
Crosscuts arrangement:
Form matka silhouette to
Express stillness in motion.

Blue Shadows—After Alina Ciuciu

Sunrise bathes with wind,
Dew, and jet spray light; marksman
Aims through small keyhole.
My dearest Foirella,
Tails' processus how exposed!!!

Shoulders' width flesh bow
Top help create a guidon
Silhouette tower.
Feet where halyard rope connect.
Bird umbra while triceps stretch.

Double-lobed Squirrel
Corn: passive flexion wings from
Pigeon's tucked upstroke.
Slide down on soft borders cause
Flinch—copy flytrap triggered.

Bow untied make a
Pose flamenco braceo
Tauro. Vaunt finest.
Panicles on Mound Lily
Yucca; daggers sans bull's blood.

Strength's flowing grace feel:
Forest spring's clean mist after

Winterstürme dark.
Breeze when all plants are in buds;
United crescendo pow.

Hold longest note in
Tune. Caelum: elegant soul
Stir with open arms.
Lachrymose euphony pass.
Compelling peafowl's vastness.

Gumnuts

Australian brass
Ensemble. Neither fibre
Optics nor mutes hang.
Chambers without stummels. Vase
Necks and carp-lips on olives.

Hollow mushroom wrench
Heads. Not sufficient for drill.
Battery operated:
Spin brush when full bloom either
Teeth or exfoliation.

Set of leprechaun's
Recycled pots-of-gold. Spell-
Bound for something more.
Eventually become
Collection of flaming worms.

Shower down to ground.
Mission is to imitate
Basketballs through hoops.
Mufflers for all Oxalis
Versicolor cane kazoos.

Ao Yem

An ancient style
Vietnamese brassiere.
Show beauty revered:
Firm, moisture abundant curves;
Cute screech on unmottled clear.

Role diversity:
Labouring along sunken
Garden on parterre,
Pose in photo session at
Curated biennale.

Bold dampness with-
Out breaking a sweat. Soaking
While collect for harvest.
Substitute for giant leaf
To clothe lady's front torso.

Kite's laces only
Around neck and centre back.
Drench with well ladle:
Glazed glue for fabric cling form
Detailed body trunk armour.

Silk handkerchief: scarf
Mini apron for model.
Where top straps come through?

Tangent centre summit tip
Or made part of smile necklace.

Collarino flesh
Dominant. Glass glow after
Fensterabzieher.
Aslant mark place for jewel:
Beacon above stomacher.

Shorn, glabrescent skin.
Clean, healthy shine nourishment.
Brume peppered with breeze.
Traditional, transparent:
Neither bark lines nor pockmarked.

Bunny pinna: her
Antitragus begins breast
Silhouette's north bound.
Fisted lotus sepals yearn
Fit pinecone concha casting.

Chokehold bud akin
To nacelle connect pylon
At fighter plane's wing.
Hub cap cone lack blades. Neither
Rotor nor turbine revolve.

Tingling onslaught
When I espy coquettish
Gadis cantik long.
Nectarean perfused crop.
Rich, fulgurate resplendence.

Spanish Gypsy

Navy blue blouse with
Layered ruffle one shoulder
Neckline; tie-up back.
Heavy ribbon glass: rotate
Trace periodic sine waves.

Seat's chiaroplane track.
Ruff's Calla lily spread dis-
Plays whipped cream sepals.
Floppy wide brim overlay.
Top nicely to make tiered skirt.

Morn's condensation,
Refulgent beams: additives
For flesh vivacious hue.
Internally galvanized:
Piezo effect fusillade.

Her passion inspires
Parasitic attitude.
Cling 'til drive matures.
Tusk-armoured bloom. Sea turtle's
Papillae from necropsy.

Arrant Beauty—After Jean Sibelius

Nostalgic grace while
Walk through gardens along path
To country schoolhouse.
No external shine to grasp
Attention. Soul-baring cherish.

Cool air condition
After pitch dark rain. Tear
Barrage renounces eyes.
Internal soar inspired by
Andante Festivo drone.

Laser drilling shock:
Invisible outpour haul
Brain, spine, heart gathered.
Vociferous summon by
Vibe builds libido acme.

Flameless backdraught felt.
Comfort after many days
Pandemic shut up.
Healing me. Sun column rouse.
Imbue after winter storm.

Sublime assuage to
Use all my senses for such
Pleasuring ration.
Wanting others to be blessed
To experience the same.

Syllabub Diffused Nymphet

Mountain peak view from
Dalat looking down foggy
Valley at sunrise.
Similar to privilege
Spanish royalty given.

Svelte Asian woman
Joins lotus pond at Hoi An.
Rain or well water:
Juices the skin foundation
With gloss taking sun's licking.

Sun douses with scan.
Rivulets trickle vacuum
Assist: hair blow dry.
Filtered flame before the kiss
Without trombone flutter-tongued.

Rondel chisel, round
Scorp hook knife: avocado
Kernel's pyrena.
Underarms' mozzarella
Texture smoothed with wire slicer.

Curves like scamorza;
Boules resting after plunge in
Ice water. Sealed tread:

Dart patch travelled by lunar
Effulgence with dampish glow.

Unvoiced plosive from
Rubbing massive amount of
Blemish balm disguise.
Devonshire Junket able
To deliquesce without miss.

Milky body cream
Base. Lacteous as if felt
Only moon all life.
Fresh bright as newly bloomed yield.
Repelled from all off-colour.

Perfume mantua
Polonaise crown shaped flacon.
Dome cap rolled upon…
Lean, firm, tight carafe figure
Hale with sleek, unctuous sheen.

Motley embellish
Sans; no soupçon green onion
In sour cream dowse.
Muscovado and coco…
Nut milk's blee and sweet fragrance.
My lambent tongue and
Touch. Soft paraffin film shield;
Lingerie night slip.
Oleaginous without drip.
Deep, internal vibrancy.

Passion's boisterous
Underset bestowed in me
By hoyden's presence.
Jugend rain proof skin perfector.
Mjukglass feast shoal unyielding.

Waves from my soul whiff
Like opening parapluie.
Tugged strings prompt sprinkles
Wet while witnessing moving
Shades from men's chorus melody…
The spirit of Myfanwy.

Erhu

Sawari: bee buzz
In distress. Dragged streaks repeat.
Loop wood slide whistle.
Gossamer trap: fly fighting
Hard but struggle to escape.

Rolling vibrato.
Bending notes while deep in thought.
Zip through sadness scales.
Sympathetic tears: doting
By fawning interjection.

Plantlets along the
Margins: fist knuckles flipped.
Wide twin step ladders.
Proximal phalanges and
Metacarpals hold swig glut.

Kalanchoe, jade plant,
Raindrop Peperomia:
Fulgent gloss foliage.
Succulent's geosmin join
In pleasant petrichor scent.

Freshen air: breathing
After rain shower where all
Allergens removed.

Gokuraku-jodo scene.
Colours vivid; smooth texture.

Sheath silhouette. Clear,
Newly bathed face caught ivory
Shaft in dead of night.
Positure chiaroscuro
Silver screen. Mien as sculpture.

Argent burrata.
On wafer cone pedestal,
Fine bone china pose.
Carriage film noir. Deportment
For dark art photography.

Entirely sheltered
In crème chantilly. Display
Antiseptic shine.
No refrigeration need.
Ćí wáwá iridescence.

Firm wishbone grips: much
Too slow to function as a
Music tuning fork.
Furcula pitch found above
Episternum—pleasure moan.
Excruciating:
At liberty to neither
Express myself nor
Pursue to satisfy my
Version of Florence Syndrome.

No imbalance to
Fall. No chimeras deceive.
No dubiety.
Corybantic sensations
Absorbed from beauty's power.

Memory reminds
Grandma's library artwork
Where she also knit.
Apricity: light stronger
Because of untrodden snow.

Coquette's Primp

Tylose powder mixed
Avoiding droop. Nub's full scope
Hermetically sealed.
Blackstrap footing every curve.
Treacle coat quintessential.

Amandine without
Crunch: how soma embedded
In a silken stole.
Sachertorte's dark hive: paste
Throng surround garash planet.

Madjarica case.
Chocolate fondant cornerstone:
Bench-scraped perfection.
Setteveli glaze fount or
Sprinkle-less brigadeiro.

Eighteenth century
Fichu tucked into bodice:
Frame caked embonpoint.
Pearl duet's satin Calla
Lily. Loops hug brachials.

Couch hides blemishes;
Décolleté plongeant cope.
Adhesive for lift.

Turban swag: scarf ends concave
Up converge neckline centre.

Esurient mood.
Abstain: famine voracious.
Near extortionate.
Torta barozzi softness
Incarnate without flaked top.

Rudiment for lust.
Deep starve fest sans tomorrow.
Throw caution to wind.
Enormous corporeal
Vehemence; spread clothe her pith.

Ripened, atomized:
Full panoply forbye one
More appurtenance.
Child refrenantem at vast
Sugar brasserie's buffet.

Zest in Florestan's
Prison cinema: month time
In isolation.
Ganzfeld: die in glory with
Heaven's angel, looks like wife.

See Through Sands at Beach

Low plunged pair of stays.
Wings tucked into neckline; silk
Fans make stretched cloud frame.
Ruffled garland streamers for
Festive wedding reception.

Periorbital puffine
Valance waterfalls too steep;
Therefore, were not used.
Appliques decorated lace.
Elegant beach silhouette.

Boat, deep V-neckline
Acting like opened oval
Squeeze rubber coin purse.
Pretty bohemian dress:
Off-the-shoulder puffy sleeves.

Third Concert Etude—After Franz Liszt's, Un Sospiro

Rain starts: separate
Bird tweets building up to down-
Pour of chirping song.
Antique tinted lithograph
Of verdaille photogravure.

Sea vaults inverted
Dimples short escape plafond.
Enervated touch:
Sporadic event caused by
Whisper hovering vellus.

Optical fibres
Squadron. Convoy formation
When eddy lines cloak.
Photophores expose swarm as
Manoeuvring cilia.

Arched breaking wave leans.
Determined with tango eyes.
Growling hunger grows.
Bioluminescence: Earth
Poles' auroras lent stained green.

Moving stamina
Treated as a sign of grace

From Almighty God.
Behaviour internally
Contrasts Laodicean.

Found anatomy
Wanting to scoosh like after
Frog in water boil.
Perfervid waves ever last
For love trigger hankering.

Magical sound: sky's
Showers land puddle fountain.
Enchanted nourish:
Drinking while barely withstand
Nestle's fierce aridity.

Approaching snake eye
Estuary. Slit outlet
Now at ramming charge.
Undertow rocking spout as
Cobra's raised posture hood flare.

If it was still: dike
Treated as unexpected
Fourchette on a glove.
Piccolo wavering trills…
Tickle focused frenulum.

Diamonds glisten when
Spotted by cloudless moonlight.
Swirl undercurrent:
Racing to shore to drop off
Gems. Set after tide recedes.

Twentieth Nocturne

Pianist performs
Chopin. Welded custom made
Domed oval arched soap.
Essential oil freshness that
Does not irritate senses.

Lighting: steam soothes her
Sinuous sculpture from mould.
Oust all soda ash.
Succulent turkey's elfen-
Bein: well rested muscles oven fresh.

Her hand reels: churning
Cyclically slow motion with
Easiest effort.
Invisible watermill's
Grace sync with sliver strokes' need.

Fingers apart skim
River surface on gibbous
Beam trail form bolides.
Across mirror water: skate
Heard in concert flute's gamut.

Flick catapults dew
Cobweb; net from golf set blasts
Simultaneous.

How presented on shirt as
Stain when trajectories land.

Great ballerina
Nocturne: virgulilla in
Hovering repeat.
Trumpeter swan curling neck:
Sculling arm for torchlight stroll.

Seeds rise on fascia,
Soffit, and eave covering
Her modillions.
Exquisite double spiral
Bookends at front and back.

Comforting giggle:
Free floating—in tempo with
Bubbles out blower.
Foam tight netted on breasts. Cause:
Languorous scrolling through ears.

Dreaming Iolanthe

Full Sap Moon appears
During my travels at sea.
See her clear, cloudless.
Thoughts spring my love moments like
These without Ceridwen fog.

Glabrate banana
Maróg set in paradigm
Altorilievo.
Right torso oxter shore bight
Resembles wide thumb web space.

Sculpture feminine:
Half of Maithuna now free
To roam around me.
Flower maiden dance: move in
Continuous twiddle waves.

Cupola's fresnel
Lens not of glass. Ideal
Degree of finish.
Panettone lighthouse tops
Anatomical snuff box.

In full health with lush
Coat. No longer under veil
Ayo yem protect.

Growth disappeared; floor brush shaved.
Groomed forest prevent fire spread.

Toothless hinged lobes span
Like stripped Dionaeas found
Under her shoulders.
Drogue tipped probe at full four-fold
Collapsible telescope.

She more than willing
Provide warm pouch when aims north
Alidade firmly.
Lens fogged. Vapour condenses:
Form puff in head blocking view.

Heaven's voice: squillo
Sublime. My attitude match
Grail's Tituel praise.
Noblest grandeur—soothing
For my soul acclaiming peace.

More Than What Meets the Eyes—Inspired by Richard Wagner

Peace with whom reflect.
Joy and comfort amongst in
Wisdom. Total blend.
Reflective thinking instead
Of living through life blindly.

Still know world beauty
And dangers. History of
The lack self-control:
Regardless changeable or
Ingrained genetic from birth.

Impromptu: take all
As it goes without worries.
Chose naivety.
Hakuna Matata mind
Taken everywhere one goes.

Disregard to void
Negative fault, pain, or see
Within one's flesh walls.
Personal desires define
And achieve: flying-boom yearn.

Wound from ambush. Lured
By conspired seduction.
Distract with lust flare.
Enough to be victim of
Steal by narcissistic hands.

Amygdala prompts
Symbolized—stab wound repeat
Tear when almost healed.
Amfortas' deep internal
Suffering always reminds.

Conscience smirch by the
Body summons though guilt is
Not truly deserved.
Degree where compassion earned.
Lesson learned: returned peace whole.

Artfoil

Hale right as rain shown.
Opaque white film's dew gloss: back
scratchboard's lingerie.
Sandwiched white china clay
Bind with black Indian ink.

Dried like settled jam
On crust. Thin layered stripes for
Scrape and cut for art.
Eschew Longinus lance mar.
Not leaving a rossaille blade.

Panel neither peg
Nor light shining through. Brush sans
Paint over-bleed drip.
Kaolin sky impression:
Imitated azuraille.

Rat Race—Inspired from Dance Choreography by Rachel Nace

I. Lady Probitas

Nurse mentality.
Aware of surroundings: will
Improvise accordingly.
Mind others' welfare; profound
Sense of empathetic charm.

Thinking others have
Same emotions will become
Victim to abuse.
Made by Opposition
Defiant Disorder brute.

Bull intimidates…
Does not surrender control.
Spin her arabesque:
Flesh in hammerhead luffing
Jib tower crane screw disguise.

Attempt intersect
Parallel universes
To help rejected.
Flip back by druggie's numb mind
Pass for push up loft ladder.

Dementing body
Drain if endured too long. Not
Being issues' cause.
Feral's intense paroxysm
Shame any backdraft forces.

II. Proper Pose

Ballerina moves
Precise like cuckoo clock. Groove
Fulfilled regardless.
Emotions mirrors reflect
Under skin—lose outside scope.

Papier-mâché lamp
Sculpture. Phial skirt for light.
Balloon dhoti stuffed:
Onion striations acting as
Hanging drupe's cage crinoline.

Pleated carnival
Merry-go-round; pixy fluff,
Whipped coconut tulle.
Digits too big for a scalp
Massage. Too thin for talons.

Came from opera house.
Sophie Mouton-Perrat's eye
For sharpened detail:
Contribute to the graceful

Pose and her costume design.

III. Overdose

Panther seen abstruse while scowl and shrivel.
Shake in pain with chronic stress for cast-off.
Struggle brings a weight expanded swivel.
Fear when miles away without a switch off.

Deep in sickness: reach as sprinkle branches.
Spread like fern-leafed frost until the river
Hyper drive makes fluid avalanches.
Hoisin sheen from balm give miry cover.

Neither booze nor scent narcotics caught need.
Can't perform routine with proper arches.
Shiver act like ambushed tact by bur-reed.
Lady Probitas' warm care approaches.

Tribal tension: trust without elation.
Lashes help in brusquely fulmination.